An Improbable Fiction

An Improbable Fiction

A comedy, mostly.

James DeVita

In Collaboration with
William Shakespeare

Words, Words, Words

SPECIAL NOTE
Anyone receiving permission to produce AN IMPROBABLE FICTION is required to give the Author credit on the title of all programs distributed in connection with performances of the play, and in all instances in which the title of the Play appears, as follows:

AN IMPROBABLE FICTION
By James DeVita
In Collaboration with William Shakespeare

The following acknowledgements must appear on the title page in all programs distributed in connection with performances of the Play:

AN IMPROBABLE FICTION was originally produced by
American Players Theater.

AN IMPROBABLE FICTION
Copyright © James DeVita
Paperback ISBN: 9781736651223

Published 2021 by WORDS, WORDS, WORDS.
Printed in the United States of America

www.jamesdevita.com

OTHER PLAYS BY JAMES DEVITA

ADULT

Christmas in Babylon
Learning to Stay
Gift of the Magi
Cyrano De Bergerac
In Acting Shakespeare
The Desert Queen
Dickens in America
Waiting for Vern

YOUTH AND FAMILY

Alex and the Amazing Lemonade Stand
A Midnight Cry
Rose of Treason
Trials: the story of Joan of Arc, and Beth
Looking Glass Land
Excavating Mom
The Thief Lord
A Little House Christmas
Treasure Island
Wonderland!
Arthur:The Boy Who Would Be King
The Prince and the Pauper
Tom Sawyer
Huckleberry Finn
Looking Glass Land
The Three Musketeers
Swiss Family Robinson

For a complete listing of Adult and Family Plays:
www.jamesdevita.com

AN IMPROBABLE FICTION was originally produced by American Players Theater in Spring Green, Wisconsin, opening on May 27, 2021. It was directed by Tim Ocel, and stage managed by Evelyn Matten. Set design was by Nate Stuber; costume design by Scott Rött; lighting design by Michael Peterson; fight choreography by Jeb Burris; the voice and text coach was Adrianne Moore; original music and sound was by Greg Coffin; costume design assistant was Kelly Meyers; and the assistant stage manager was Lorely Dedrick. The cast was as follows:

Mistress Quickly	Sarah Day
Falstaff	Brian Mani
Messenger	Ronald Román-Melendéz
Othello	Chike Johnson
Cleopatra	Tracy Arnold
Juliet	Melisa Pereyra
Understudies	Janyce Caraballo, Rasell Holt
	Jess Lanius, John Phillips
	Tim Gittings

AN IMPROBABLE FICTION

CAST

Sir John Falstaff
Mistress Quickly
Messenger
Othello
Cleopatra
Juliet

If this were played upon a stage now,
I could condemn it as an improbable fiction.

-- *Twelfth Night*

Evening. The Boar's Head Tavern, Eastcheap, London. Early 1600's during the time of the plague. There is an outside door to the tavern which opens inward. Inside, we see a bar, a table, and chairs. At the back of the room are stairs which lead up to a railed landing, off of which there is a bedchamber.

At rise, MISTRESS QUICKLY *is behind the bar cleaning, keeping a watchful eye on* SIR JOHN FALSTAFF *who is sitting in a chair, staring off.*

Pause.

Falstaff sings softly, melancholily.

FALSTAFF

O, MISTRESS MINE, WHERE ARE YOU ROAMING?
O STAY AND HEAR, YOUR TRUE LOVE'S COMING,
BANISH NOT THIS OLD HEART SO.
TRIP NO FURTHER, PRETTY SWEETING:
JOURNEY'S END IN LOVERS MEETING,
EVERY WISE MAN'S SON DOTH KNOW . . .
EVERY WISE MAN'S SON DOTH KNOW.

Pause.

QUICKLY

Excellent good, i' faith.

Pause.

FALSTAFF

Time?

QUICKLY

But new struck nine

FALSTAFF

Ay me, sad hours seem long. *(Pause.)* A pox o' the plague! What, shall we have no more cakes and ale? No laughter? No love? Faith, I can still cut a capon, and the mutton to it! Shall we raise the night-owl, love? *(He grabs her and they dance.)* Come, let us chime the chimes of midnight and make the welkin dance!

QUICKLY

Oh, Sir John! Sir John!

FALSTAFF

THERE DWELT A MAN IN LONDON TOWN,
OF REPUTATION GREAT WITH FAME.
HE TOOK TO WIFE A LOVELY LASS,
MINE HOSTESS WAS SHE CALLED BY NAME.
A WOMAN FAIR AND TRUE WAS SHE . . .

QUICKLY

Oh, Sir John! Ha, ha!

FALSTAFF

LADY, LADY!
SO GIVE ME DRINK, AND GIVE ME SONG,
LADY, LADY!
A MERRY HEART LIVES HAP'LY LONG,
LADY --

The tavern door suddenly opens. A MESSENGER *rushes in.*

MESSENGER

Pardon me, my lord.

FALSTAFF

Cease!

MESSENGER

But --

FALSTAFF

Halt!

MESSENGER

But --

FALSTAFF

Speak not, reply not, do not answer me.

MESSENGER

But there's a --

FALSTAFF

Draw thy *speech* to a close *(draws his sword)*, or thus will I draw and quarter *thee. (Keeping him at swords length.)* Very well then, approach. Near enough. Who art thou?

MESSENGER

Who art I?

FALSTAFF

'Tis I asked you.

MESSENGER

Who art I.

FALSTAFF

By heavens, he echoes me -- go to, go to, you are a saucy boy. Come, villain, thy place, thy position, character, role, capacity -- divulge, impart, speak!

MESSENGER

I, uh, I --

FALSTAFF

Convey, sir; what's your will?

MESSENGER

I've a message for you, sir.

FALSTAFF

From whom?

MESSENGER

The Author.

A brave pause.

FALSTAFF

(Falstaff slowly sheathes his sword.) Thou comest to use thy tongue; thy story quickly.

MESSENGER

Oh, I don't have a story, sir. I just bring the news. From abroad.

FALSTAFF

I see. And who art thou?

MESSENGER

Who do you want me to be?

FALSTAFF

Dost mock me, villain?

QUICKLY

He means the play, lad, what play are you from?

MESSENGER

Oh, oh. Well, uh -- all of 'em, actually. *(Beat.)* You don't know me, do you?

FALSTAFF

Damned if I do, thou surly-mouthed, beetle-headed, flap-eared, knave. Never in my life have I spied the likes of you.

MESSENGER

(With humility and respect.) Ay, I know. You never notice me. I've watched you all your life, sir, but ye've never said a word to me.

FALSTAFF

I never -- ? Why, thou misbegotten bat-fowling bootlicker -- who are you, goodman boy? Thy name.

MESSENGER

I don't 'ave one, sir. Not in particular, that is.

FALSTAFF

Elucidate, brazen-face!

MESSENGER

Well, uh, you may have heard of me. I'm actually pretty well known throughout the canon as 'The Messenger'. THE Messenger, that is -- not just one of, you know, those every-day messengers. Very important character, mind you. Without those messages, you know, nothin' happens. I am also, at times, uh, Soldier, Servant, Gentleman, Officer, Shepherd, Sentry, Sailor, Citizen, Page, Serving Man, Clown, Musician, Eunuch, and other Attendants.

FALSTAFF

Extensive. Unremarkable, but extensive. Come, boy, your message now relate -- *(with hopeful expectation)* -- is it about the Prince?

MESSENGER

Nay, my lord, no -- the Privy Council's passed a new decree, sir . . .
The playhouses are all to be closed.

QUICKLY

Closed?

MESSENGER

Aye, madam, and to stay closed until the numbers rise not above
thirty a week. The Lord Mayor himself has made the proclamation.

FALSTAFF

A plague upon't!

MESSENGER

Precisely, sir, and gettin' worse: the entire canon is to be closed, sir.
They've locked the doors o' The Globe, The Rose, The Curtain --

FALSTAFF

The Blackfriars?

MESSENGER

Ay, sir; and the Fortune and the Swan -- all of 'em sealed up tight as
oak.

FALSTAFF

Then where be my compatriots? Where is Bardolph and Master
Shallow? Why are they not here? And what of Marlowe's characters?
Webster's and Middleton's?

QUICKLY

I'll 'ave none o' Webster's characters in my place!

FALSTAFF

Peace, I pray you!

MESSENGER

I know not about Bardolph and Master Shallow, sir, but Marlowe and his characters 'ave been passin' the time at Mistress Bull's house in Deptford.

QUICKLY

And Master Shakespeare?

MESSENGER

Oh, he's been shut up at his place over on Silver Street. Runnin' about like a madman, he is, scroungin' paper, ink. He's got a new play ticklin' his brain, something on a heath somewhere.

FALSTAFF

How fares great Tamburlaine? Were lies Volpone? ZOUNDS! I am barren and bereft of friends, and you may know by my size that I require a like quantity of companions. It's not the damn plague will kill me, it's the solitude. Where the hell is Hal!?

QUICKLY

Now, Sir John --

FALSTAFF

Banished I am of my Harry's company -- why?

QUICKLY

John.

FALSTAFF

Tell me that, Mistress! Tell me that! Not a word from the boy!

QUICKLY

Best not to dwell upon such things.

FALSTAFF

I'll dwell upon this theme until my eyelids no longer wag!

QUICKLY

Come, come, and sit you down, you shall not budge.

FALSTAFF

(He sits.) I cry you mercy. I am parched for companionship. Which pains me greater than -- Tell me, lad, tell me . . . the other characters . . . do they . . . do they ask after me?

MESSENGER

Oh, indeed they do, sir, never fear that. Ay, if there was ever a man to last out a siege like this with, it'd be Sir John Falstaff, that's what they say: Parson Hugh and Pistol, Poins, Peter Simple.

FALSTAFF

Know you their whereabouts?!

MESSENGER

Indeed, sir, they're at Mistress Bull's too.

FALSTAFF

What the devil do they all in Deptford?! Are we not consanguineous? Nearly? Our house has not been marked.

MESSENGER

No, it's not that, sir; marry, they closed the bridge over at Bankside. Master Marlowe can't get out of Deptford either. He stays at Mistress Bull's now, and he's been usin' his time there to revise Tamburlaine a little bit.

FALSTAFF

Blasts and fogs upon it! *I* need no revisions! The Merry Wives and I are most obscenely and courageously prepared -- even Master Ford is on the cheer about it.

MESSENGER

But there's nowhere to gather, Sir John; it's been decreed 'n posted. Every theater is closing, the streets are almost empty save for the Watchmen and their carts come nightfall; and there's nary a physician to be found, they're all leaving the city.

QUICKLY

Winters not gone yet if the wild geese fly that way.

MESSENGER

I do have some good news, though.

FALSTAFF

Say you?

QUICKLY

Ay?

MESSENGER

Master Shakespeare wants to take Merry Wives out on tour.

FALSTAFF

Oh, ye gods.

MESSENGER

Out in the provinces, away from the crowds, he might still be able to get a play up. The horses are all dead, but it's only a three day walk.

FALSTAFF

On the hoof, say you?!

MESSENGER

Ay.

FALSTAFF

I'd rather be set quick i' the earth and bowled to death with turnips.

MESSENGER

Well.

FALSTAFF

I abhor touring! Three days walk, indeed. Eight yards of uneven ground is threescore and ten miles afoot to a man of my kidney. 'Sblood, I'll not have my flesh borne so far afoot for all the coin in the king's exchequer. Let William write some other character into a buck-basket and see how they like it!

MESSENGER

Master Shakespeare's meetin' with the Lord Mayor right now, tryin' to get a license. He's not a penny left, sir, and nothing comin' in on account of the closures.

FALSTAFF

Tour and be hanged!

MESSENGER

But the rent is due, my lord. The actors have to eat, they've no place to sleep.

FALSTAFF

Actors never needed food or sleep before! Just a crowd, an open space, and words.

MESSENGER

There are no crowds allowed, sir!

FALSTAFF

ZOUNDS!!!

MESSENGER

We might lose the theater, Sir John.

Pause.

FALSTAFF

The Globe. Our wooden O?

MESSENGER

Ay, sir. It's that bad. Something's got to be done.

FALSTAFF

. . . Unless we have the Globe in which to sing,
There is no music in the nightingale;
If we lose the world of stage on which we play,
There is no world for us to look upon;
It is our essence.
   (Beat.)
Of course. Of course, I'll do the tour.

Falstaff moves off. Pours himself a drink.

QUICKLY

Is it true, son? About the Globe?

MESSENGER

I'm afraid so, mum.

QUICKLY

How come's it you know all this?

MESSENGER

I'm the messenger.

Falstaff suddenly, and violently, kicks over a chair.

QUICKLY

Now, now, Sir John, keep you heart high. The theater will outlast
this blasted plague.

FALSTAFF

Yea, but will I?

QUICKLY

We've been through bad times before, love.

FALSTAFF

Never like this.
Never, never, never, never, never.

QUICKLY

Come now, my melancholy knight. Let us embrace adversity bravely, eh? Like smug newlyweds. *(Falstaff smiles.)* Ay, there's my Sir John. We'll ne'er wail our losses, but seek their remedies.

MESSENGER

(Earnestly.) Ay, heaven help us that way.

QUICKLY

Look not to the heavens, lad, nor the crown. We've to help ourselves now. They at the court care none for us -- never 'ave.

FALSTAFF

Damn their eyes! A stoup of wine, say I, and LIVE! *(Offering drink to the Messenger.)* Come, lad, thou lack'st a cup of canary.

MESSENGER

Uh, thank you, no.

FALSTAFF

Pourquoi, my boy? Wherefore should these delights be forsworn?

MESSENGER

Oh, I uh, I just don't -- no. Thank you, though.

FALSTAFF

Want of experience, lad. Want of experience.
Come. I will instruct thee.
    (Falstaff takes a large swallow of his drink.)
AH! A plague o' the pox!
AND LET ME THE CANNIKIN, CLINK -- CLINK!
AND LET ME THE CANNIKIN CLINK!
    (He encourages the messenger to join in with him.)
A SOLDIER'S A MAN, *(Messenger shyly joins in.)*
MAN'S LIFE'S BUT A SPAN!
WHY THEN LET A SOLDIER DRINK--

The front door of the tavern swings and OTHELLO *rushes in.*

FALSTAFF

How now, General.

OTHELLO

Say you now, was she at Emilia's?

QUICKLY

No, my lord.

OTHELLO

The Citadel?

QUICKLY

No.

OTHELLO

The Sagitarry?

QUICKLY

No.

OTHELLO

Death and damnation!

FALSTAFF

She did range the town to seek her out, milord.

OTHELLO

Her father, he was not at home.
Where might he be, think you?

QUICKLY

Nay, I know not.

MESSENGER

(A tentative step forward.) . . . uh . . . Pardon me, sir . . .
The senator's are all in council, good my lord.

OTHELLO

Say you?

MESSENGER

'Tis true, my lord. Her father, Signor Brabantio,
Hath summoned the meeting himself.

OTHELLO

In council at this time of night?
Upon what cause?

MESSENGER

The great folk are all leaving the city, sir --
Senators, Magistrates, their sons 'n daughters,
All of them -- till this pestilence is passed.

OTHELLO

I received no word. How know you this?

MESSENGER

I'm the messenger.

OTHELLO

I do fear . . . Her father hath been ever opposite
To our marriage -- if he hath taken her . . .

FALSTAFF

By heavens, has he ought to do with this,
I'll so carbonado his shanks! *(Draws.)*

OTHELLO

Put up your sword, Sir John; if I once stir
Or do but lift this arm, the best of them
Shall sink in my rebuke.

Othello starts out.

QUICKLY

Come, sit thee down, my lord.

OTHELLO

Nay, the affair cries haste, and speed must answer it.
  Othello exits, Falstaff calling after him.

FALSTAFF

Ask after Hal if you -- ! *(Othello's gone.)* Blasts and fogs upon it!

Falstaff sits to rest, Hal still very much on his mind.

QUICKLY

I tell thee true: Desdemona deserves a better father than Signor Brabantio. *(Closing the door to the tavern.)* And that that man should bear the name of Senator!

FALSTAFF

I'd beat him, but it would infect my hands.
  (A sudden thought strikes him.)
He's at the Mermaid!

QUICKLY

Brabantio?

FALSTAFF

No, Hal! Prince Hal! I'll lay fourteen o' my teeth
He's at the Mermaid.

QUICKLY

Sir John, please, *please*, you must cease harping on that string.

FALSTAFF

But he's not at the Bankside or The George,
Or the Tabard Inn or the Lamb and Flag --
Ye've yet to seek him at the Mermaid!

QUICKLY

He's thrown off his looser ways, Sir John; you know that. His father
is near to --

FALSTAFF

I shall seek him then myself!

Falstaff grabs his cloak and makes to leave.

QUICKLY

You're not going out there, John, you're not well -- John!

FALSTAFF

Step aside, woman.

QUICKLY

I'll not step aside!

MESSENGER

He's not at the Mermaid, sir!
   (Falstaff stops. Beat.)
Prince Harry.
You will not find him there.

FALSTAFF

How know you that?

MESSENGER

I'm the messenger.

FALSTAFF

(Cutting him off.)
Then where is he, if you know so damn much,
You thin-kidneyed rascal?! Why isn't he here?

QUICKLY

Why would he be, Sir John? You know it is not meet that Hal should here be seen. In such a time as this, and his father so sick as he is. How many young princes would do the like? John. You must stop thinking he is the thing he was.

FALSTAFF

Ay, Ay, I know! . . . he'll be one o' the 'great folk' soon.
   (Beat. Then rallying.)
He shall send for me in private, you shall see!
Ay, my whole heart weeps for the wretched cub,
For he must act this part t'the world and seem
Thus aloof from me. Poor boy. I'll write him!
   (Aloud as he cogitates.)
"Sir John Falstaff, knight, to the son of the king:
Harry Prince of Wales. Greetings."
   (To himself.)
I shall be sent for soon at night.

The door flies open and CLEOPATRA *bursts into the room.*

CLEOPATRA

WHERE THE HELL IS HE?!

FALSTAFF

Of whom do you speak, my Queen?

CLEOPATRA

You know damn well of whom I speak, John,
Play not the fool with me!

QUICKLY

What's the matter, lovey?

CLEOPATRA

ANTONY! ANTONY!
What is ever the matter, but Antony!
Where lies he now? With Fulvia? Octavia?
Charmian, perhaps?

FALSTAFF

Cleopatra --

CLEOPATRA

The goddamn Soothsayer? I wouldn't put it past him.
Does anyone know his whereabouts?

QUICKLY

Nay, madam.

FALSTAFF

(Of the messenger.) He might.

CLEOPATRA

Oh, why did I think he would be mine and true,
When he hath played me false an hundred times ere now!

FALSTAFF

Most sweet queen.

CLEOPATRA

Most false love! Cut my lace asunder, Mistress --
Quickly! -- Ay, that my pent heart may have scope to beat!
Oh, my oblivion is a very Antony!
    (Noticing the messenger.)
Who is that man there?

QUICKLY

Oh, he's, the --

CLEOPATRA

I've seen him somewhere before.

QUICKLY

He's the messenger, madam.

CLEOPATRA

He is?

MESSENGER

I am.

CLEOPATRA

You're expository, yes?

MESSENGER

Well, I prefer to think of it as --

CLEOPATRA

You know all.

MESSENGER

Well, not really -- but a bit.

CLEOPATRA

Then you have news; else why art thou in my presence?

MESSENGER

'Tis true, madam. I do have news.

CLEOPATRA

Of Antony?

MESSENGER

Ay, madam.

CLEOPATRA

Oh, speak then!

MESSENGER

(Gravely.) Madam, forgive me, for the news I bring is . . .

CLEOPATRA

Bad. Very bad. Oh, God, my mind misgives
Some vile forfeit of his untimely death.

MESSENGER

Stay, madam! Antony is --

CLEOPATRA

Dead! Dead for a ducat! I knew it!

MESSENGER

Madam --

CLEOPATRA

If thou speak it aloud, villain, I'll unhair thy head!

MESSENGER

Madam, Antony is --

CLEOPATRA

AHH!
> *Cleo lunges at the messenger. A chase ensues.*

FALSTAFF

Cleopatra, hold!

MESSENGER

Madam, please!

CLEOPATRA

Oh, horrible, horrible, most horrible!
Villain thou shalt be whipped!

MESSENGER

Madam, if you'll but hear me. Antony is very much --

CLEOPATRA

Dead! Very MUCH dead! Oh!
Melt Egypt into Nile and kindly creatures
Turn all to serpents! Oh, I faint! Iras! Charmian!

QUICKLY

They're not here, madam.

CLEOPATRA

Tis no matter.
Husband, I come! Pity me, Isis --

MESSENGER

Madam --

CLEOPATRA

Nay, do not speak to me!

FALSTAFF

Good lady, keep yourself within yourself,
And hear the lad speak.

CLEOPATRA

(Beat.) I am tame, sir. Your news. Come. Pronounce.

QUICKLY

He's afeared to speak, madam.

CLEOPATRA

I will not hurt him. Approach, boy.
Though I am sharp, I will not bite.

MESSENGER

(Frightened.) Madam, to punish me for sayin' what you would make me say, I feel is most unequal.

CLEOPATRA

I cry you mercy. Though it be honest,
It is never good to bring bad news.

MESSENGER

But I bring no bad news, Madam.

CLEOPATRA

How say you?

MESSENGER

Madam, Antony is alive.

CLEOPATRA

Oh, heavens be praised!

MESSENGER

And he's well.

CLEOPATRA

Sweet, sweet music to my ears!

MESSENGER

He is very, very well.

CLEOPATRA

Better and better still!

MESSENGER

But yet, madam . . .

CLEOPATRA

I do not like 'But yet.'
Fie upon 'But yet.'
Speak all or I'll have thy tongue.

MESSENGER

(Delicately.) Antony is very much alive, Madam -- as I said -- 'n he lies at Mistress Bull's house in Deptford with, um, Master Marlowe, and Tommy Dekker, and uh, well, (john), and Beaumont and Fletcher and --

CLEOPATRA

John, did you say? John who?

MESSENGER

Webster.

CLEOPATRA

John Webster. Is the Duchess with him?

MESSENGER

The Duchess, my lady?

CLEOPATRA

Of Malfi.

MESSENGER

. . . Ay, Madam.

CLEOPATRA

AHHHH!

Cleopatra goes for the Messenger. Another chase ensues. Ad-libbing as needed. While this is happening, the door slams opens and Othello enters. He pays no attention to the mayhem in the room, but goes straight to the bar and grabs a bottle.

MESSENGER

(Mid-chase.) 'Tis no fault of mine, madam! I'm just the messenger!

Cleopatra's fury subsides. Somewhere she crumples. Mistress Quickly goes to help her. Falstaff goes to Othello. Messenger has no idea where to go.

QUICKLY

(Comforting Cleo.) There, there now, Egypt.

FALSTAFF

(To Othello, at the bar.) How fared you, my lord?

OTHELLO

(Of the bottle.) This is empty.

Falstaff gets another bottle as Cleo speaks to Mistress Quickly.

CLEOPATRA

(To Quickly.) O, Nell, Nell, what a falling off was there.
That it should come to this? Heaven and earth,
Must I remember? Why he would hang upon me
As if increase of appetite had grown

By what it fed on, and yet . . .
Let me not think on't -- frailty, thy name is Antony.

QUICKLY

Consider it not so deeply, love.

CLEOPATRA

First was there Lady Montague, then Bianca,
Adrianna of Ephesus, and now
This Amalfi woman -- Italians!

QUICKLY

My Queen --

CLEOPATRA

He cannot call it love, for at his age,
The hey-day in the blood is tame, it's humble
And waits upon the judgement; and what judgement
Would step from this *(gesturing to herself)*, to such a thing as --

*Othello angrily breaks away from the bar -- mid argument with
Falstaff.*

OTHELLO

If she be false, then heaven mocks itself,
I'll not believe it!

FALSTAFF

I said not 'false,' my lord,
But bound, perhaps -- by chains of obedience.

OTHELLO

My life upon her faith!

CLEOPATRA

(Acknowledging him for the first time.) My lord.

OTHELLO

My Queen.

CLEOPATRA

I did not notice you.

OTHELLO

No, you did not. *(Sits away.)*

FALSTAFF

(Gesturing to Cleo to excuse Othello's mood.) He's a little, uh . . . just .
. . -- Drink?

CLEOPATRA

God, yes.

FALSTAFF

A stoup of wine, Mistress

*Falstaff and Cleopatra join Othello as Mistress Quickly pours Cleo
a drink.*

CLEOPATRA

What is it, General? What has happened?

OTHELLO

My wife. My wife. I have no wife.

CLEOPATRA

Oh, god, Desdemona -- dead?

OTHELLO

Ay, to me; or so they would have her be.
She is taken from the Sagittary,
Under pretense of the plague, by special
Officers of night -- who 'sought her safety' --
Taken from the city I know not where!

QUICKLY

Marry, can they do that?

OTHELLO

Ay, 'tis too true an evil.
Emilia at the Citadel I met,
And she hath told me all: the Senate
Hath approved the action; the nobility
All are fled; and the poor, having no choice, remain.

FALSTAFF

As Desdemona, having no choice,
Perhaps was forced to flee.

OTHELLO

Ay, ay . . . I cannot think that she would leave
On her own accord.

QUICKLY

I tell thee, Brabantio her father, he's to blame! A man who hates
upon no better ground but that he hates.

OTHELLO

Her father loved me. The Senate loved me.
The consuls, magistrates, and soldiers loved me.
Every time there was a need, they loved me.
Every time there was a war, they loved me.
No color could they see were there battles I could win.
No, then was I the noble Moor, the valiant Moor,
The adored and gracious, worthy Moor!
O, most false affection: loved not for what I am,
But only for what I can do -- yet, could I bear this;
Well, very well; I have done so all my life:
And yet when I did dare to love of theirs --
My soul's joy -- my gentle Desdemona --
This they could not bear; and ever since,
With faithless eyes and forced smiles,
Suffer they my service.
Her father alone, in his hatred, is honest.
Their love is sin.
O, what may man within him hide,
Though angel on the outward side!

FALSTAFF

Devils all! By my troth, it makes me mad.
I am sorry for this, my friend.

OTHELLO

Sorry is not sufficient!
    (Beat.)
By heaven, my blood begins my safer guides to rule,
And passion leads the way. Forgive me, John.
Rude am I in my speech, and little blest
With the soft phrase of peace; for from the womb --
Whether at war or no -- this battle
Is all I have ever known.
This news outrages you, you say; and yet to me,
It is my rise of sun and set of day.

    (Beat.)

CLEOPATRA

. . . Emboldened by plague and a lawless court,
Such men no longer hide their poisoned hearts.
The vows of senators, lovers, and kings,
Melt away, *these* days, as breath into the wind;
An infectious ill-dispersing wind,
Scouring away all but a kind of truth, perhaps . . .
Exposing . . . what once was merely hid:
Those who truly care . . .
And those who do not . . .
And those who never did.

In a pause, the messenger tentatively steps forward.

MESSENGER

Um, 'scuse me. Sir? General? *(Othello glares at him.)* Pardon me, sir,
I don't mean to, um -- it's just that --

OTHELLO

Speak, boy!

MESSENGER

You dropped this over by the bar, sir.

The Messenger holds out a silk handkerchief spotted with strawber-
ries.

OTHELLO

. . . Gentle heavens.
   (He takes it.)
I thank you.
   (Short pause.)
This handkerchief did an Egyptian
To my mother give; it is bewitched:
A sibyl that had numbered in the world
The sun to course two hundred compasses,
In her prophetic fury sewed the work;
The worms were hallowed that did breed the silk.
My mother told me, that while I kept it,
'Twould bring good health and fortune of the Gods.
She dying, gave it me.
To lose it were such perdition as nothing else
Could match -- chaos would come again.
   (A curious beat.)
I have known thee e're now, boy, have I not?

MESSENGER

. . . Yes, sir.

OTHELLO

From whence?

MESSENGER

Cyprus, sir.

OTHELLO

Thy name?

MESSENGER

In Cyprus, sir, I am Cypriot Gentleman number four.

OTHELLO

Ah, yes, yes: Act 2, scene 2; the fight
With Iago and my lieutenant:
As I enter the fray, Cassio hits,
With the wiggen bottle, your head.

MESSENGER

Ay, sir. That's me.

OTHELLO

Very well-spoken, that scene; with good accent
And good discretion.

MESSENGER

Ye-yes, sir. Yes. Thank you, sir!

OTHELLO

(Beat.) You may go away now. (Messenger retreats.)
This fellow's of exceeding innocence,

And doubtless sees and knows more -- much more --
Than such as you and I.

FALSTAFF

Well. He's the messenger.

The door of the tavern opens and JULIET *enters. She slams the door, angry, and remains above, gripping the railing, silent.*

JULIET

Ay me. . .

   Pause.

FALSTAFF

(To Quickly, quietly.) Shall I hear more, or shall I speak at this?

JULIET

Fie. Fie.

CLEOPATRA

(Stepping in, carefully.) How do you, lady? *(No answer from Juliet.)*

QUICKLY

What, lamb? What, ladybird?
What Juliet!

JULIET

Forgive me, mistress, my thoughts are far
From where I abide.

FALSTAFF

What is it, Jules?
What make you here at this hour?

JULIET

A troubled mind drove me to walk abroad --
And yet, to whom should I complain?
Did I tell this, who would believe me?

OTHELLO

Who hath wronged thee, child?

FALSTAFF

Be it the Montagues again? By heaven,
I'll shake the muddy-mettled-rascals by the ears.
Fetch me my rapier, boy!

JULIET

Forebear, good uncle,
'Tis no Montague that grieves my heart so.

FALSTAFF

Who then, Juliet?

JULIET

My father! Who else should it be?
Ever and always, my father.

FALSTAFF

Oh, Old Capulet again?

JULIET

Ay, and worse now than e'er he was before:
His tyranny, together with his jealousies,
Torment me so, that if within his prison walls
I abide another minute more, I surely
Shall run mad.

QUICKLY

Prison, my lady?

JULIET

My house is a prison!

OTHELLO

So is the world, then, these days.

JULIET

Aye, a goodly one, in which there are many
Confines, wards, and dungeons, my father's
Being one o' th' worst.

CLEOPATRA

Say, Juliet, what is it hath passed between
Thy father and thee?

JULIET

NOTHING! For 'tis he alone
Who says all, does all.

FALSTAFF

Come now, Juliet.

JULIET

I'faith, 'tis true! I begged him with humble patience
But to hear me speak -- his reply?
"Talk not, reply not, do not answer me!"
Again and again, refusing to lend an ear
Unto my wishes; bidding me do
Only that which he has set down for me.
Oh, these men. These men!
Ever and anon endeavoring to fashion
Our lives according to their desires.

CLEOPATRA

(Thinking it's about Romeo, teasing.) Oh ho, and what are your desires, Juliet?

QUICKLY

(Teasing too.) Nay, methinks I know what they are -- ah? I know that which vexes Capulet so. Come now, tell your aunty true, my love, where is thy Romeo?

JULIET

Oh, Romeo, Romeo!
Wherefore am I only ever asked about Romeo!
Can I not be written a single scene
In which our names are not entwined as if we're twins?
Knows't thou not I possess a life of my own!
Wants of my own! Much to the surprise of my father --
And the world, it seems.

QUICKLY

We were only askin'.

JULIET

Day, night, work, play,
Alone, in company -- Romeo, Romeo!
And if not that, it's my father's cry of Paris!
'Valiant' Paris! 'Summer's flower' Paris!
Ever and anon, his only care hath been
To have me matched, as if I were a china dish,
Worthless until made a set!

FALSTAFF

Do you not give him thanks?
Are you not proud? Do you not count yourself blest
That he hath wrought so worthy a gentlemen
To be your bridegroom?

JULIET

Proud can I never be of that which is imposed
Upon me -- I am no weaker vessel, I.

FALSTAFF

These are wild and whirling words, girl!

JULIET

If I chance to talk so wild, Uncle,
Forgive me -- I had it of my father.

FALSTAFF

Will you speak ill of him that hath raised you?

JULIET

Shall I speak well of him that would enchain me?

FALSTAFF

You deny your father and his good name
Thus to disobey his will!

JULIET

With all my heart I do! I'll obey my own will
Or I swear, I'll no longer be a Capulet!
Lay hand on heart: I'll beg, starve, die i'the streets,
Ere bend a knee unto his purposes!

QUICKLY

Too hot, too hot! *(Stepping in good-naturedly to stop the argument, concerned about Falstaff exerting himself too much.)* Tilly-vally, loves! Tilly-vally! Fie, how the both of you relish a good skirmish. But enough wrangling now, I say. Come, I cry a match.

JULIET

(Pause.) I cry you mercy, good uncle.
My tongue must tell the anger of my heart,
Or else my heart, concealing it, will break;
And, rather than it shall, I must be free
Even to the uttermost, as I please, in words.
    (Beat. Falstaff's focus drifts slightly.)
I must be gone. My father will search the town
If he finds me not at home.

OTHELLO

I should be gone as well, Mistress.

CLEOPATRA

And I.

FALSTAFF

Yet stay but a little? Friends. I do beseech thee! *(Turns his desperation it into a joke.)* Why I . . . I've not cheated anyone at cards in eleven days. Great talent should never rust unburnished, but shine in use. *(Beat.)* Yea, and mark me this: Prince Hal is sure to be here on the hour, the jack-a-napes. *(Mistress Quickly clocks this.)* And when he doth appear, it shall be sport for all, for I will devise matter enough out of his absence to keep him -- and the lot of you -- in continual laughter enough to last out the plague. I say, stay if you love me!

CLEOPATRA

Laughter indeed would be a welcomed sound.

JULIET

If I stay, good uncle, you may have to answer to old Capulet.

FALSTAFF

Upon my life, I shall -- or send the mistress.

OTHELLO

(To Cleopatra.) I thought the prince was with his father?

FALSTAFF

Come, let us crack a quart together!

Falstaff drags over a chair or two, or perhaps pushes two tables together, so they can all sit. Since entering, none of the visitors have really 'settled.' If there are cloaks or swords still on, they now come off.

Mistress Quickly eyes the messenger.

QUICKLY

Why so quiet, lad?

MESSENGER

When my cue comes, I will answer it.

QUICKLY

(A curious beat.) Well, while you're waitin' for it, best make yourself useful. Come 'n help here.

Mistress Quickly and Messenger pass cups/wine.

CLEOPATRA

(Of the drink.) Another for me too, Nell; to remedy my nerves.
Feel you, General, feel how I shake, look you;
As if 'twere a very aspen leaf.

OTHELLO

What sadness is it grieves your majesty?

CLEOPATRA

Not having that, which having, grieves me more.

QUICKLY

'Tis her Antony again.

OTHELLO

Oh. I am sorry for it.

JULIET

And what of Desdemona, my lord, how fares she?

OTHELLO

She too is suffering her father's house.

FALSTAFF

Let us give the cheer!

Glasses raised, Falstaff takes note of the messenger, who has been rather indiscernible for a time now. The messenger will do this throughout the play: whenever not in a scene, he retreats to the periphery somewhere -- unobtrusive, engaged, attentive, observing -- like good messengers are wont to do; always putting his focus where the story needs it to be, and not on himself.

FALSTAFF

Hold! *(Glasses lowered.)* You, young sir. Yes, you. Master Silence. Be not afeared of greatness; I pray you, come and crush a cup of wine with us.

MESSENGER

Thank you, no, my lord. I cannot.

FALSTAFF

What -- what is that word . . . can-not?

MESSENGER

Forgive me, my lord, but I have very poor and unhappy brains for drinking. I could well wish courtesy would invent some other cus-tom of entertainment.

FALSTAFF

So would not I. Well, to each their own discretion. *(Turning back to the table, he toasts.)* To better days! Clink, clink!

They drink: "Here. Here's," perhaps and such ad-libbing. Falstaff, trying to lighten things up even more, offers up a card game.

FALSTAFF

Come, my friends. Let's hazard a game of cards to cheer the time. I've not beaten the General since last we played.

OTHELLO

You have not *cheated* the General since last we played.

FALSTAFF

Oh, that was but a foolery. I would never actually do so with friends -- *(Objections from the table -- in fun -- no one trusts him.)* Very well, very well -- we shall play at dice then. *(Greater objections.)* See me here, now: I stand like a man at a mark, with a whole army shooting at me. So be it, I capitulate. *(He rises to get cards from behind the bar.)* We shall -- *(he suddenly doubles over slightly, grimacing)* -- ah, ah, 'tis nothing, nothing -- an old wound. We shall toss a hand of Primero! *(Rallying with humor.)* And let the gods here witness, I shall not cog or cozen, but play honestly. If I can remember how.

Mistress Quickly has risen to see if Falstaff is alright. He gently shoos her away: "It's fine. I'm alright," etc., and continues on to get the cards.

CLEOPATRA

(Privately.) I like not that.

OTHELLO

Nor I.

JULIET

Is he ill?

QUICKLY

He hath been.

JULIET

Is it . . . ?

QUICKLY

No, no, love. It's not that.

CLEOPATRA

What is it then?

FALSTAFF

(Returning with a drink and cards.) Come now, let us play!

JULIET

 I shall pass.

FALSTAFF

Oh, come, I'll teach thee, Jules. Thou'lt be the wiser for it.

JULIET

I am wise enough, good uncle, to know not to play with thee.

Falstaff deals. The table plays cards. Perhaps a card term or two punctuates the game. Juliet, who had noticed the messenger earlier, now approaches him.

JULIET

I know you.

MESSENGER

My lady?

JULIET

When first I entered, I knew you.

MESSENGER

Yes.

JULIET

I've seen thee at my father's house.
You're Musician number 3, aren't you?

MESSENGER

Ay, my lady. My scenes are often cut
These, days -- but, ay, I am.

JULIET

What are you doing here?

MESSENGER

. . . I'm the messenger.

JULIET

And you're the musician.

MESSENGER

I am. I am whatever is needed.

Whenever it *is needed*. At your father's house,
I'm the musician. *Actually*, I'm the singer.

JULIET

And what is it that you sing, Musician number 3?

MESSENGER

I sing Heart's Ease, my lady.

An enigmatic beat between the two of them . . . broken by --

CLEOPATRA

Fluxus! *(Lays her cards down.)* Ha, ha! On my first hand! Fluxus for 70! Ha, ha!

OTHELLO

You have bettered me, my lady. I do resign. *(Tosses cards in. Cleo enjoys this.)*

QUICKLY

(Completely lost.) I've no idea a'tall how to play this game -- resign! *(Cleo enjoys this too, assuming she has won.)*

FALSTAFF

(Rising.) A moment, a moment -- *(laying his cards down)* -- a *Chorus* of Sevens -- for 84!

CLEOPATRA

84?! *(All react in disbelief-- a very difficult hand to get.)*

OTHELLO

Was ever man had such luck.

QUICKLY

Aye, aye, the luck of a highwayman, perhaps.

FALSTAFF

Upon my Knighhood, 'twas dealt me! *(Reactions.)*
Doubt not, my minions! I have grown honest
This past -- hour.

QUICKLY

Then is doomsday near.

The good-humored dispute begins to slide slightly southward for Cleopatra, who is feeling her drinks now; not so much angry at first so much as nettled.

CLEOPATRA

True, true. To be honest as this world goes
Is to be ten men picked out of a hun . . . a man --
One -- a hundred men out of --

OTHELLO

One man picked out of ten thousand.

CLEOPATRA

That!

FALSTAFF

Ay, and that one honest man stands before thee now!

CLEOPATRA

Excellent falsehood! You've packed the cards and underplayed my glory. As did Antony, and Caesar, and my father before him, and then my brother Theos -- well, he *tried* to, at least, but . . . well, we wont talk about that. Dost hear, Juliet? Thou art not alone, child, in thy paternal-la-listic woes. Speak'st thou of thy father's house? My father was a king. Now there's trouble in the palace. Then I married Caesar -- and beshrew me, those Julii can be, well, overbearing would be a nice way to put it -- and I didn't marry him for his affections, mind you, but for the power of the Roman legions that came along with him. But of course, Master Shakespeare didn't write me any such scenes as those; no, no, much more interested in my running around like a love-sick schoolgirl chasing after Antony for three and half hours. Why, by Isis, in my salad days I spoke nine languages, was schooled in mathematics, philosophy, oratory, astronomy, bore four children, lead a naval fleet into battle, and ruled a kingdom for 22 years! And thanks to that damned play, what am I remembered for today? Antony and an asp.

JULIET

Forgive me, your Majesty, but heaven knows
You need not suffer it as you are wont to do.

CLEOPATRA

(A chilly beat.) Pardon me, my child, do not presume
Upon our friendship. I do not suffer it.
I do not suffer anything. Or anyone.
I am rendered as the Author intends.

JULIET

Well, if that's true, then . . . *(an idea blooming more clearly within her)* . . . alter the rendering.

FALSTAFF

What say you?

JULIET
(Confirming it for herself.) Yes. Alter it.

A courageous pause.

CLEOPATRA
That's absurd, child.

JULIET
Why? Why is it absurd?

QUICKLY
(Bewildered.) Alter it?

JULIET
Of course.

MESSENGER
How?

JULIET
Change the words.

OTHELLO
That -- what . . . that is not possible.

JULIET
Why not?

CLEOPATRA

Because we . . . well, because . . . these are the words,
The words we've been given -- they're our script.

JULIET

They are *his* words and *his* script.

OTHELLO

But they are both the same, child.

JULIET

No they are not --
And everyone please stop calling me child!
These words -- that literally shape our lives --
Were imagined by another, by an author,
But we need not be bound by them. *(Pointedly to Cleo.)*
Yes, all the world may be a stage, but we must stop
Acting as if we're merely players upon it.

MESSENGER

Yes!

CLEOPATRA

I am no mere player!

The argument escalates quickly into real anger.

JULIET

Of course you are. You said so yourself.

CLEOPATRA

I did not!

JULIET

'Rendered as the Author intended,' you said; 'underplayed' by Caesar, your father, Antony, your brother --

CLEOPATRA

Speak not of Antony!

JULIET

All you're known for is Antony!

CLEOPATRA

That's not true!

MESSENGER

(Thinking he's being helpful.) But that is what you just said, madam.

CLEOPATRA

Dare'st wag thy tongue at me, villain!? AH!

Cleopatra lashes out, once again, at the messenger.

QUICKLY

Your majesty!

JULIET

He does nothing but speak true!

Pursuit, ad-libbing, as Mistress Quickly tries to step in.

QUICKLY

That's quite enough now -- I'll not have this in -- I'll not 'ave any --
all of you, please -- I SAID THAT IS ENOUGH! *(This is a sound
we have not yet heard from Mistress Quickly, very different from her
otherwise upbeat and maternal energy. All stop to listen. Tough love.)*
That shall suffice. *(Beat.)* Now listen to me. I don't know much
about the workings o' this world . . . 'specially not now with it o'er-
turned topsy-turvy as i'tis. I don't understand this talk about al-
terin's and renderin's and changin' o' words. I've no schoolin', I run
a tavern, and never get paid. I don't 'ave a play named after me. And
I only ever speak prose. Yet this I do know: this is no time for friend
against friend. I'll not have it. *(Pause.)* We all have our hurts -- and
they are not slight.

Pause.

FALSTAFF

You are in the right, dear Nell.
You are in the right.

Beat.

OTHELLO

Come, let's have no more of discord and dismay,
The world provides quite enough of that today.

*Silence. A noticeable pall still remains in the room. Falstaff, sensing it,
draws his sword, dramatically.*

FALSTAFF

Othello, my friend! Come, let us play!

OTHELLO

Play, my lord?

FALSTAFF

Ay, play a match with me to shake off this great frost
Of misery. *(All hesitate a moment.)* I say, we shall play!

*Chairs and tables are pushed aside -- perhaps begrudgingly at first.
Falstaff begins warming up, humorously overplaying his age and ail-
ments. As the scene progresses, all, in time, are won over, and start
to laugh with more ease.*

FALSTAFF

(Warming up with feigned -- or real -- difficulty.) The keys, my
friends, to maintaining -- a -- *ah* -- a healthy physique -- such as mine,
is -- resist, Cleopatra, resist -- *oo!*-- are the rich advantages of good ex-
ercise -- and a -- *ow* -- regiment of daily practice . . . in the art of de-
fense. AH!

*Falstaff takes a lunge, from which he cannot rise. Juliet and Cleo step
in to help -- all in fun.*

FALSTAFF

Thank you, my ladies, thank you.
   (An afterthought, or so he pretends it to be.)
By the mass, I had forgot me:
Hast either of thee in thy wanderings
Heard aught of my mad wag, the prince?

JULIET

I have not, Uncle.

CLEOPATRA

Nor I.

FALSTAFF

Ah, by my troth, I care not! The Prince is a Jack!
And he were here I would cudgel him like a dog;
For the snipe cannot move a man to laughter
More than a joint-stool!
   (Laughter from others.)
He hath no more wit in him than a mallet.
   (More laughter. He takes a last big stretch.)
There now! My mortal preparation is complete.

OTHELLO

(With laughter.) Come, come, my friend, we are too old for such dallying.

FALSTAFF

Old, say you!? *(Falstaff, performing, tries to touch his toes.)* Why this young trunk of mine hath yet the very pith of life in't!

OTHELLO

Can'st see the toes thou'rt striving for, Sir John?

FALSTAFF

Ay, goodman-wit, I see them -- feelingly.

QUICKLY

Lie down then, lovey, 'n see if that helps!

FALSTAFF

Have you any levers to lift me up again, being down?

CLEOPATRA

(Near tears laughing.) Alas the day, good heart, this is excellent sport!

FALSTAFF

Weep not, sweet Queen, for trickling tears are vain.

CLEOPATRA

Ha!

FALSTAFF

For god's sake, friends, convey my tristful Queen
For tears do stop the floodgates of her eyes.

Othello and Falstaff, swords out, begin to circle.

QUICKLY

Don't break anything, Sir John!

FALSTAFF

Fear not, sweet wench, I am lithe and limber.

QUICKLY

I mean the furniture, John!

FALSTAFF

Come, sir, begin. And you the judges, bear
A wary eye.

They play a bout. It is very fun, friendly throughout. Othello clearly the better of the two.

OTHELLO

One!

FALSTAFF

No!

OTHELLO

Judgement.

QUICKLY

A hit!

JULIET

A hit!

CLEOPATRA

A palpable hit!

MESSENGER

Ay!

FALSTAFF

Well, sir, again.

CLEOPATRA

I'faith, Sir John, you're as red as any rose.

FALSTAFF

Flushed with victory, that is all, my Queen! Have at you now, sir.

They play again. As they do, others begin to notice that Falstaff doesn't seem himself. He is quickly winded and flushed.

OTHELLO

(Trying to end the match.) A hit. A hit.

FALSTAFF

Ay, ay, I do confess it. Come, again.

OTHELLO

Nay, Sir John.

QUICKLY

I' faith, love, ye've drunk too much canaries.

OTHELLO

As have I, Sir. I beg thee, John, give me leave to rest awhile.

FALSTAFF

What, just as I have thee! Nay, come again, sir. Why, I am barely breathed.

Messenger attempts to step between them.

MESSENGER

(Concerned.) Barely breathed? Why, Sir John, you can barely move.

                    FALSTAFF
Out of my way, boy.

                    QUICKLY
Leave 'em be, son.

                    FALSTAFF
(To Othello.) Come, sir! *(They en garde positions again.)*

                    MESSENGER
(To Quickly.) But he's no room for breath in that ancient bosom, madam -- *(Falstaff is about to begin the bout)* -- it's all filled up with midriff.

   Falstaff suddenly turns on the messenger.

                    FALSTAFF
Ha? Wherefore?

                    MESSENGER
Sir?

                    FALSTAFF
What say you?

                    MESSENGER
Nothing.

                    FALSTAFF
Dost thou mock me, boy?

MESSENGER

I? No -- *no*, my lord!

OTHELLO

Come, John.

FALSTAFF

(Still on the messenger.) What said you then? Say't again.

JULIET

Uncle Jack.

QUICKLY

He was only trying to help, John.

MESSENGER

I -- I meant no offense, my lord! I, I -- I was just --

FALSTAFF

(Abrupt shift of tone now -- pleasant -- pretending it was a joke) Ay, ay, ay, 'tis no matter, no matter, lad -- I do but *jest*! Ha, ha! No, no offense i' th' world. *(He takes up another sword and politely offers it to the messenger.)* Come, my young sir. Will you play a match with me?

MESSENGER

I -- I sir?

FALSTAFF

Ay, you, *you* sir.

MESSENGER

But I . . . I'm just the messenger here, sir.
I -- I've not been written into a fight.

FALSTAFF

Well, let's just *'alter'* that, shall we?
Let's just . . . *amend* things, as we see fit.
Is not that of interest to you?
I heard thee say even now it was.
(Putting sword in his hand.) No Author need guide our hands.
So. There you are. Now. Have at me, boy.

MESSENGER

My lord, I cannot.

FALSTAFF

I pray you.

MESSENGER

Believe me, I cannot.

FALSTAFF

I do beseech you.

MESSENGER

I know no touch of it, my lord.

FALSTAFF

It is as easy as mocking. Grasp thou the pommel with your fingers and thumb, thus; give it motion with thine arm, and it will thrust and parry most effectively.

MESSENGER

But this I cannot command to any semblance of proficiency, my lord
-- forgive me, I cannot play!

FALSTAFF

Why look you now, how unworthy a thing
You make of me. You would play upon me,
You would seem to know the breadth of my worth,
You would pluck at the heartstrings of mine age;
You would scorn me in my lowest days,
At the height of mine infirmity;
And there is much skill, much death in this little
Instrument, yet cannot you make it sing?
  Draws his sword again.

'Zounds, here's my fiddlestick. Here's that shall make you dance!

Othello, weapon in hand, steps between them.

OTHELLO

Put up your sword, Sir John!

*Falstaff, with a burst of agility, disarms Othello, and quickly has his
sword to the Messenger's throat.*

FALSTAFF

Thou unthinking, unmannered, unexceptional, boy. There was
once much spirit, much vigor, joy, life, skill, strength, expertise and
expectation in this old grayness of mine. The glory of my youth may
be on the wane, but not my heart. Yea, I am not now of that strength
which in the old days could move hearts and fell men; that which I

am, I am; made weak by time and fate, but strong in will to survive, to seek, to live, and not to yield. Call me what you will, though you fret me you cannot play upon me --

Falstaff is unexpectedly taken with a fit of coughing. He drops his sword and stumbles toward the stairs, clearly fatigued from the exertion. Cleopatra and Mistress Quickly rush in to help him.

QUICKLY

I prithee help.

MESSENGER

He's feverous and doth shake.

QUICKLY

Take him upstairs -- please.

Cleopatra and Othello help Falstaff up the stairs and into the bed-chamber. Juliet runs up ahead of them to open the door. Mistress Quickly grabs some towels and heads up.

MESSENGER

(Calling after her.) I . . . I didn't mean it. I'm sorry

QUICKLY

'Tis better playing with a lion's whelp than an old one dying.

MESSENGER

Dying? Is it -- ? I mean . . . ?

Mistress quickly stops, looking down at the messenger.

QUICKLY

No, no. It's not the plague, young sir . . . the the Prince has killed his heart.

She continues up and enters the bedchamber.

Juliet grabs her cloak and a sword/belt and starts out.

MESSENGER

My lady?

JULIET

I do remember an apothecary,
And hereabouts he dwells.

MESSENGER

But --

Juliet rushes out of the tavern.

The messenger, unsure of what to do, wanders a bit.

He picks up a few things and puts them back in place. After a moment, he spies the deck of cards left on a table.

He picks them up.

End of Scene One

SCENE TWO

Later, early a.m. The messenger at table, flipping cards before him. He mutters quietly to himself, trying to remember how to play Primero.

MESSENGER

Ace, six, seven . . . Maximus. *(Othello enters from bedchamber. He remains above, the messenger, not noticing him.)* Four of the same suit . . . Fluxus. *(Flips out more cards.)* Four of a kind . . . a Chorus. Two of the same suit . . . two of the same suit . . .

OTHELLO

Two or three of the same suit is called a Numerous.
'Tis the worst hand one can draw.
  (Preoccupied, he starts down the stairs.)
Queen Elizabeth, I am told, is unusually
Fond of the game; she once did take Lord North
For forty pounds. And his horse. *(He sits, troubled.)*

MESSENGER

My lord?

OTHELLO

  (Beat.)
The web of our lives, young sir, is as a mingled yarn,
The good and bad together . . .
  (Beat. Trying to occupy the time.)
Come, I will teach thee to count; *(deals cards)* . . . two through five
Count ten, plus their own worth. Thus your four, counts
Fourteen. King thru Jack are worth ten --

CLEOPATRA

(From within.) Juliet! Juliet!

OTHELLO

(Realizing she's missing.) Where is Juliet?

CLEOPATRA, *paper in hand, enters from the bedchamber. Sleeves rolled up, apron or towel wrapped around her waist, she's a bit tousled from having nursed Falstaff through the night.*

CLEOPATRA

Where is Juliet?

MESSENGER

Gone.

OTHELLO

What mean you gone?

MESSENGER

She said she knew of an apothecary hereabouts.

CLEOPATRA

What apothecary? Where?

MESSENGER

I know not, madam.

OTHELLO

None abide but in the heart of the city,
Where the disease doth reign the greater.

CLEOPATRA

Fie, this is too rash, too sudden, too unadvised;
At this hour, the night's breath is most contagious.

Othello gathers his things and starts to leave.

OTHELLO

More than the plague do I fear for Juliet;
Concealing night is when men most do tyrannize,
Without regard for person or degree. *(At the door.)*

CLEOPATRA

You must not leave till morning now, when heaven's eye
Hath power to cleanse the air.

OTHELLO

How long hath she been gone?

MESSENGER

Some time now.

OTHELLO

(Decides its best to wait.) Heaven keep her safe.

CLEOPATRA

(Handing Othello the paper.) I pray you, lend a hand.
Nell was given that of Dr. Caius once,
May be it will the fever ease.

OTHELLO

(Reading.) "Sage, rue, briar leaves, and elder leaves."

MESSENGER

(Helping to look for ingredients.) How does Sir John?

CLEOPATRA

Very ill, i'faith. In the heaviness of sleep
We bathed him and put fresh garments on him,
But the fever lingers. It will not break --
I know there's rue here.

OTHELLO

"A quart of white wine."

MESSENGER

That we have. *(Places a bottle on the bar.)*

OTHELLO

"Ginger, and honey."

CLEOPATRA

Here's elder, but I see no sage.

MESSENGER

I found some honey.

CLEOPATRA

There's no briar, no sage, nor ginger -- now by Apollo,
We've not half here of what is needed!

OTHELLO

Aqua vitae and chicory set with lemons,
Did my mother give.

MESSENGER

Violet and strawberry leaves mixed in almond milk, my --

CLEOPATRA

We've a tavern here, not the blasted London market!
I'm sorry. I am sorry.
So oft my fears convert to anger.
Beshrew these unhelpful tears! Like Niobe.

MISTRESS QUICKLY *enters from the bedchamber.*

QUICKLY

(A bit frantic.) Any luck, love?

CLEOPATRA

Little. *(Of the remedy.)* Half, at that.

QUICKLY

Bring it up then; make use o' what we can.

Cleo gathers up the items. Mistress Quickly perhaps gets some more towels and/or basin of water, etc.

OTHELLO

Has the fever left him?

QUICKLY

No, poor John, he's still so shaked of a burning. His heart is fracted, sure. *(Starting back up.)* He asks for a song; only for song and sack he asks.

MESSENGER

I can play.

QUICKLY

Can you?

MESSENGER

Aye: Musician number 3. Act 4, Scene 5. Juliet's Chamber. Among other plays.

QUICKLY

There, in the cabinet.

MESSENGER

What tune, Mistress? I know 'em all.

QUICKLY

(Hurrying back up.) What you will, lad, what you will.

Othello stops Mistress Quickly.

OTHELLO

May't please you, Mistress, tender this to Sir John.
  *(He takes out his mother's handkerchief and holds it carefully in his
    hands.)*
My mother bid me once, if ever Fate
Should show me brother or sister more in need
Of it than myself, 'tis I, then, should give it they.
So please you now, I offer it Sir John.
  (He places the handkerchief in her hands.)
Take heed on't: there's in the web of it.

QUICKLY

Indeed, I'll give it him, my lord.

OTHELLO

It is required we do awake our faith.

QUICKLY

Ay, my lord. *(To Messenger.)* The song, sir.

Mistress Quickly and Cleopatra exit to bedchamber.

MESSENGER

(Quietly playing the melody.) This is Act 2, scene 5, As You Like It. My character is a little hard to see in that scene, but I'm in there -- to the left o' the second sycamore. William writes: "Enter Amiens, Jacques -- and Others." That's me: 'Others.' And, mind you, I am not like some o' those clowns who say more than the Author actually sets down for them -- no, tha's not me. For there be 'o them that will themselves laugh, to set on some quantity of barren spectators to laugh too; though, in the mean time some necessary question of the play be then to be considered. That's 'villainous' -- that's what Master Shakespeare says -- and shows 'a most pitiful ambition in the fool that does it.'

Cleopatra rushes out of the bedchamber.

CLEOPATRA

By Juno and Jupiter too-- the song!

MESSENGER

Ay, Ay. Sorry. Sorry. Here i'tis.

Cleo exits.

MESSENGER

Sorry.

OTHELLO

Warble, my son; make passionate his sense of hearing.

MESSENGER

(Sings.)
UNDER THE GREENWOOD TREE
WHO LOVES TO LIE WITH ME,
AND TUNE HIS MERRY --

A loud commotion is heard coming from Sir John's chamber. Mistress Quickly enters.

QUICKLY

Peace, lad, peace! Another tune, he likes it not!

MESSENGER

A love song or a song o' good life?

QUICKLY

Nay, he cares not for good life -- something bawdy! *(She exits again.)*

MESSENGER

DO NOTHING BUT EAT, AND MAKE GOOD CHEER
AND PRAY TO GOD FOR A MERRIER YEAR;
WHEN DRINK IS CHEAP AND FRIENDS ARE DEAR,
AND LOVES ARE FOUND BOTH FAR AND NEAR,
BE MERRY, BE MERRY, FOR LIFE IS ALL!

SO DO ME RIGHT AND DUB ME KNIGHT
FILL THE CUP, AND LET IT COME;
I'LL PLEDGE YOU TO THE BOTTOM!
SAY, HEY, A MERRY HEART LIVES LONG!
DO NOTHING BUT SING AND DANCE THE HALL,
AND WOO YOUR LOVES BOTH SHORT AND TALL;
'N TREASURE THE DAYS YOU CAN RECALL
OF THOSE WHO DID YOUR HEART'S ENTHRALL.
BE MERRY, BE MERRY, FOR LIFE IS ALL!

SO DO ME RIGHT AND DUB ME KNIGHT
FILL THE CUP, AND LET IT COME;
I'LL PLEDGE YOU TO THE BOTTOM!
SAY, HEY, A MERRY HEART LIVES LONG!

OTHELLO

Well played, young sir, well played.
(Tries to tip him.) There is for thy pains.

MESSENGER

(He politely refuses it.) No pains, sir, I take pleasure in singing.

OTHELLO

I'll pay thy pleasure then.

MESSENGER

Truly, sir, and pleasure will be paid one time or another.

A curious pause between them...

JULIET *enters, breathless, wearing the sword which she had taken on her way out earlier.*

JULIET

Oh, break my heart. Poor bankrupt, break at once.
On all sides is sorrow; everywhere is fear --

OTHELLO

How is it with you, madam?

JULIET

The thing we see before our eyes pierces
Further and prints deeper into our hearts
And minds, than that of which we only hear.

OTHELLO

Come. Sit. Sit. Didst find the apothecary?

JULIET

Ay.
His needy shop now a vast silent charnel-house,
Hung with dark lamps dimly glimmering
In its hollow corners. What unmatchable
Torment must it be to be barred up there within --
For so the unfortunate were. Here, a boy,
Thickly mingled with the heaps of the dead;
The bare ribs of the father that begot him,
Lying near beside; here the chapless hollow skull
Of the mother that bore him -- God save the mark --
Pale, pale as ashes; I swounded at the sight.
On the streets, the speechless Watchers are about;

No noise but the trundling of plague carts
Over cobblestone, carrying the dead to graves;
The air, everywhere oppressive, full o'the stench
Of death and corruption; and then --
Oh god, man, proud man -- most ignorant
Of what he's most assured, infused with self
And vain conceit, performs such acts before
High heaven as make the angels weep --
I saw, then, a throng of the multitude, defying
Curfew, and the law, and all compassion,
Pressing so near to others on the street,
Strewing the venomous contagion about,
Wandering heedless through lanes, on corners, in taverns --
Merciful Heaven!
What a blemish on our fair nation;
For it hath spotted our country with the stain
Of cruelty and disregard; this,
The subtle vapor of indifference,
Kills more than the disease.

OTHELLO

Indeed, it distempers the mind as horribly
As plague does the body.
I am sorry you had to see this, Juliet.

JULIET

How will posterity ever believe
That once there was a time like this?
Oh, happy people of the future,
Who will never know these miseries,
And class our story perchance with fables . . .

Oh god . . .
I have an ill-divining soul . . .
My father. Methinks I see my father . . .
Before I left, we -- *(Starts out again.)*

OTHELLO

Juliet.

JULIET

I need to return home.
See well to my uncle.

OTHELLO

Juliet, hold!

JULIET

I will not, sir.

OTHELLO

It is not yet day; wait for the sun to show itself.

Othello steps between Juliet and the door. She draws.

JULIET

Do not bar my way, good sir!

OTHELLO

Look you! I have known battles and sieges;
Accidents of flood and field, and hair-breadth scapes
In the imminent deadly breach of war.
This is but another battle. This I know.
Allow me council.

JULIET

Speak, my lord.

OTHELLO

Here we are yet well. Here we are yet safe.
We have each other. All this is comfort. Yes?
Now. In the morning, early, after the sun
Hath cleansed the new day's air, I myself and --
What is your name?

MESSENGER

I don't 'ave one, sir.

OTHELLO

I and the messenger will escort
Thee to thy father's house.

JULIET

And if it then be sealed and I shut out?

OTHELLO

'Tis almost morning, Juliet -- an hour more
Is all I say; if danger there is to face,
See it better by the day.

JULIET

I have a faint cold fear thrills through my veins.

OTHELLO

As do I, Juliet. Never battle has there been,
Where, before the like, I have not felt the same.

Juliet puts down her sword.

Cleopatra enters, towel over her shoulder, basin in hand.

CLEOPATRA

Juliet! Thank heaven you are safe returned.
The apothecary, now, what said he?
Can he minister to a heart diseased?

JULIET

To him I spoke not, madam.
Seeing it was a house where the infectious
Pestilence did reign, I did not dare to enter.
The Watchers, having marked and sealed the doors,
Eyed me as I turned to leave, and suspecting
I had been in the house as well, pursued
Me halfway down to Cheapside Lane.
Escaped I did by nary a breath
Or they'd have sealed me in too.

CLEOPATRA

Good heavens.

JULIET

How does my Uncle Jack?

CLEOPATRA

Scarce half-awake.
Resting, yet still weak and fever-shaken.
Juliet starts up the stairs to the bedchamber.

CLEOPATRA

'Tis best, I think, we let them alone awhile.

JULIET

I hope all will be well.

Pause.

MESSENGER

(Trying to be helpful.) The tour might be good for Sir John. *(A 'look' from all.)* Out i'the country, I mean, in the open air 'n all. They say it's good for you.

OTHELLO

Tour? What mean you tour?

MESSENGER

Oh. Master Shakespeare's puttin' together a tour of Merry Wives.

OTHELLO

Not Othello?

MESSENGER

Uh, sorry, sir, no.

OTHELLO

Why -- why is this?
Thinks he I can make a life of complacency?

MESSENGER

Oh, no, it's not that, sir, it's just that Merry Wives, well, all ya need is a couple o' chairs, table, and a buck basket; and for Herne's Oak, we use wha'ever woods they got there; but with Othello, you got Cyprus, Venice; Venice, Cyprus; the Venetian and Cypriot costumes; senators; we got wiggen bottles -- it's just too much to lug along.

CLEOPATRA

Well, thank the gods it's not Antony and I;
We'd devour each other e're the first night's call;
I'd rather go Roman and swallow hot coals.

JULIET

I can't believe touring to be such a hardship.

CLEOPATRA

At your age, my dear, of course you cannot;
Trust me, the allure dissipates. Quickly.
I was toured for 15 years in my day,
With a scant 12 actors and a brace of juvenile
Hirelings picked up along the way,
To play 66 characters and 34
Speaking parts in 42 scenes; and then,
For the Battle of Actium, a burnished barge
Which literally burned on the water. Every night.
Thank you, no. I'm quite content to wait
Until the theaters reopen again.

The action is interrupted by loud hammering on the front door. Every-one freezes. The hammering continues. When it stops, the messenger carefully opens the door. There is now a large RED CROSS *painted across it, with a* PAPER NOTICE *nailed over it. The messenger takes down the notice and reads.*

OTHELLO

Pray, sir, what read you?

MESSENGER

Mine own fortune in our misery.

OTHELLO

I mean what you see.

MESSENGER

It reads: LORD HAVE MERCY UPON US.
(Beat.) There'll be no leavin' here now.

CLEOPATRA

Why so? There is no contagion here.

The messenger peers out the door.

MESSENGER

They need only suspect, madam.
They've got Watchers stationed at every corner --
And they're armed.

OTHELLO

Let me see.

JULIET

How may this be prevented?

MESSENGER

It may not, madam.
Confined we are till further direction be given.

JULIET

My father shall grow sick with fear,
He knows not where I am.

CLEOPATRA

How long will it last, think you?

MESSENGER

That's up to the Privy Council, my lady.
Eight, ten days -- could be as much as forty.

JULIET

Oh, God.

CLEOPATRA

We've not food enough for forty days.

MESSENGER

We can entreat more food o' the Watchers.

OTHELLO

Say you?

MESSENGER

Place we what coin we have in a bowl o' vinegar,
And set it outside the door.

OTHELLO

How know you that?

MESSENGER

I'm the messenger!

OTHELLO

(Beat.) Juliet, these forty ducats take of me.
(To Messenger.) Boy, discern thou the provision of water.
(To Cleo.) My lady, get me some ink and paper;
I'll draw the form and model of our charge.

As everyone busies themselves, Mistress Quickly enters from the bed-chamber and stands silent on the upper landing. As each person notices her, they stop.

Pause.

QUICKLY

Bristle thy courage up; for Falstaff he is dead.

Pause.

OTHELLO

Is it e'en so?

JULIET

Can heaven be so envious?

QUICKLY

Ay, that it can. His immortal part with angels lives. He made a finer end and went away an' it had been any christom child; he parted even now: for after I saw him fumble with the sheets and smile upon his fingers' ends, I knew there was but one way; for his cheeks were pale as lead, and he babbled of green fields. 'How now, sir John!' quoth I 'what, man! be o'good cheer.' So he cried out 'God, God, God!' three or four times. Now I, to comfort him, bid him he should not think of God; I hoped there was no need to trouble himself with any such thoughts yet. So he bade me lay more clothes on his feet: I put my hand into the bed and felt them, and they were as cold as any stone; then I felt to his knees, and they were as cold as any stone, and so upward and upward, and all was as cold as any stone. He cried out for sack, he did. And a song.

Beat.

CLEOPATRA

There's a great spirit gone.

QUICKLY

He never lifted up his voice but people laughed.
He was too full of life to live long.

OTHELLO

What words are left me? His spirit exceeds my speech.

JULIET

We shall not see the like of him again.

The bedchamber door suddenly swings open and Falstaff bursts out.

FALSTAFF

Do not think so, you shall not find it so! *(A huge laugh from him.)*
HA, HA, HA!!

*He is wearing a night shirt now, and has Othello's handkerchief tied
around his head.*

QUICKLY

God save us!

OTHELLO

What's this?

CLEOPATRA

Praise, Isis.

JULIET

Heaven bless us!

QUICKLY

Sweet, sweet, sweet, honey lord!

CLEOPATRA

And they say miracles are past!

OTHELLO

The HANDKERCHIEF!

QUICKLY

But I saw thee breathless and cold, pale as lead!

FALSTAFF

Tut, tut, my love, 'twas but my time to counterfeit! Or that hot termagant of a tapster death had found me sure 'n pressed me for payment -- 'tis not due yet! I would be loath to pay him before his time!

JULIET

If this were played upon a stage, I would condemn it as an improbable fiction.

QUICKLY

I thought thou hadst left me, John.

FALSTAFF

Nay, nay, a death-counterfeiting slumber, t'was all it was. *(Suddenly remembering a dream he'd had.)* . . . If I may trust the flattering truth of sleep, my dreams presage some joyful news at hand. I dreamt that Hal returned and found me dead -- strange dream, that gives a dead man leave to think -- and breathed such life with laughter into my heart that I revived and was an emperor. Ha, ha!

CLEOPATRA

Hark, how hard he fetches breath.

FALSTAFF

Why, look you! Here comes the rascally wag now!

Falstaff is speaking to the air. There is no Prince Hal before him.

FALSTAFF

Ha, ha! HAL! HAL! God save thee, sweet boy! My prince! My Jove!

QUICKLY

Alas, Sir John, how is't with you, that you do bend your eye on vacancy?

FALSTAFF

(To the image before him.) I knew thou wouldst ne'er deny my love!

OTHELLO

He knows not what he says: and bootless 'tis
That we present thus to him.

QUICKLY

John, John, whereon do you look?

FALSTAFF

Why, on . . . on . . .

Falstaff falters, the vision before him fades. He is lost now, bewildered. He starts to collapse -- the messenger steps in to help him -- as Falstaff looks at him, he now believes the messenger to be Prince Hal.

FALSTAFF

On him! On him! HAL, my boy! Ha, ha! Oh, you rogue, you. Come closer, boy!

The Messenger steps closer, remarkably Prince-like now. Falstaff turns to Othello.

I told thee, Master Shallow, did I not, I would be sent for in private by him? Ha, ha! He disavowed me not. Look you -- he will be King here one day, so in public he must seem to stand aloof from me. *(To Messenger.)* Hal, my heart's life, where hast been, lad? I should chide thee horribly for vexing me so. Ay, father-like, as I have always been to thee, I shall examine thee on the particulars of thy absence, thou heart ruiner, thou. Ha, ha! Thy father is a King, is he not? As am I, in this my dominion of companions -- *(to all)* -- yea, thou, and thou, and thou, yea all of thee be the riches of my kingdom. Canst thou . . . *(Having noticed his change of shirt, he loses his way again. He turns to Mistress Quickly.)* . . . Pray, do not mock me, but all the skill I have remembers not these garments, nor do I know where I did lodge last night.

QUICKLY

We're at the Boar's Head, John -- oh lord, your hands are ice cold.

FALSTAFF

Ay, that's well said, Master Ford; a good heart's worth gold.

QUICKLY

Juliet, his cloak.

FALSTAFF

Ay, fetch me my robe! I have immortal longings in me! *(He addresses Cleopatra and Mistress Quickly.)* Mistress Page. Mistress Ford. My sweet dears, my does; setting the attraction of my good parts aside, would you be so kind as to help a foolish, fond, old man. *(Juliet places the cloak on Falstaff's shoulders. Cleopatra and Mistress Quickly help him to sit down.)* This shall be my chair of state. *(He calls to Othello.)* Bardolph! Give me a cup of sack to make mine eyes look red, that it may be thought I have wept for my wayward son; for I must speak in passion --

Falstaff is distracted suddenly by the sight of Juliet.

. . . You are a spirit, I know; where did you die?

JULIET

Uncle Jack, dost thou know me?

FALSTAFF

To speak plainly, I fear that I am not in my perfect mind. Methinks I should know you, but I am doubtful. Pray do not laugh at me, for, as I am a man, I think this lady to be Lear's child, Cordelia. Ah! Be your tears wet? I pray you, weep not, my nightingale. Though I am mightily abused, know that I shall chastise my wayward one-time son. Stand aside, nobility! *(Everyone obeys Falstaff and moves off -- everyone except the messenger, who remains a stand-in for Prince Hal.)* We are amazed, and thus long have we stood to watch the fearful bending of thy knee because we thought ourself thy lawful king. *(Messenger kneels.)* Harry. Harry. I do not only marvel where thou spend'st thy time, but also how thou art accompanied; yea, in what villainous fellowship thou dost pass thy days. And yet, there is a very virtuous man I have often noted in thy company, but I know not his name.

MESSENGER

What manner of man, an it like your majesty

FALSTAFF

(Unable to remember.) A goodly portly man, i' faith, and a corpulent; of a cheerful look, a pleasing eye, and a most noble carriage; and, as I think, his age some fifty, or, by'r lady, inclining to three score; and now I remember me, his name is . . . his name is . . .

MESSENGER

(Gently.) Falstaff.

FALSTAFF

Falstaff. So it is. Harry, I see virtue in that man. Thou shoulds't with him have kept and banished all the rest. Tell me now, thou naughty varlet, tell me, where hast been? Ungracious boy, deny'st me thy love for my age? That I am old, the more the pity, these white hairs do witness it; but that I am less the friend because of it, that I utterly deny. If sack and singing be a fault, God help the wicked! If to be old and merry be a sin, then many an old host that I know is damned. If to covet friendship be a vice, then I am the most offending soul alive. If to be fat is be to be hated, why then 'tis a fault 'gainst heaven, for 'twas heaven created me as I am. No, my boy; banish illness, banish piousness; banish falsehood, hatred and hypocrisy: but for sweet Jack Falstaff, kind Jack Falstaff, true Jack Falstaff, valiant Jack Falstaff, and therefore more valiant, being, as he is, old Jack Falstaff, banish not him thy Harry's company, banish not him thy Harry's company: banish plump Jack, and banish all the world.

Beat.

MESSENGER

I do not. I will not.

Messenger kisses Falstaff's hand.

FALSTAFF

Why, is not this, then, all? Now art thou what thou art: my son, my Icarus, my blossom. *(Suddenly distracted, he shouts at a new vision that begins to pester him.)* Get thee gone, villain! I have been drinking all night; I am not fitted for it. *(To the messenger.)* Indeed, Hal, thou hast redeemed thy lost opinion and showed thou mak'st some tender of my life in this fair rescue thou has brought me. *(To the vision.)* Avaunt and quit my sight! There'll be a time for such a word tomorrow! *(To Messenger.)* You do look, my son, in a moved sort, as if you were dismayed. Be not disturbed by my infirmity, 'tis but my revels which now are ending, and this -- *(gesturing to his body, his hands)* -- this is all spirit, and will soon be melted into air, into thin air; and, like the baseless fabric of this vision, shall fade and then dissolve; as must we all, for we are such stuff as dreams are made on. *(To the vision)* Oh, very well, very well! you crook-pated pester-y rascal. You shall have gold enough to pay the debt twenty times o'er! *(To Quickly.)* My reckoning, Mistress! It is a heavy one, but well spent. Ha, ha! *(To Messenger.)* I would 'twere bed-time, Hal, and all were well. *(He rises and confronts the vision.)* Ay, ay, enough of your endless prattle, you moldy rogue, you! Nay, do thou amend thy face, and I'll amend my life! Why, I was as virtuously given as a gentleman need be. Swore little; diced not above seven times a week; drank too much once in a quarter -- of an hour; paid money that I borrowed, three of four times; lived well and in good company -- mostly. Nay, nay -- you to your work, and I to mine, and there's the rendezvous of it! *(He turns back to Messenger, who he no longer sees as Hal.)* Give us a song, lad! Give us a . . . who are you?

MESSENGER

. . . I'm the messenger.

FALSTAFF

(He sees something completely different in the boy now.) Ay, that you are, lad, that you are. *(Quite lucid now.)* There must be conclusions, eh? *(Beat.)* Then sing to me the while, my good he-Mercury, sing.

MESSENGER

A love song or a song of good life?

FALSTAFF

A love song, a love song. I've had a good life.

MESSENGER

Which one, my lord?

FALSTAFF

That piece of song, that old and antic song
You played, to which I cried 'no more';
Some things seem sweet now, which were not so before.
Come, but one verse.
   (Messenger begins to strum quietly.)
Mark it, mistress, it is old and simply sung;
It dallies with the innocence of love,
And the days of splendor -- when we were young.

Mistress Quickly helps Falstaff sit.

Ah, Nell, give me thy lips! Is it not strange that desire should so many years outlive performance? Ha, ha! By my troth I kiss thee with a most constant heart. Farewell, mistress. *(They kiss.)* Fear not, sweet chuck, I am a fiction I cannot die.

QUICKLY

Sweet John --

FALSTAFF

Sh, sh, sh. Let be. Let be. I go to it merrily. Sing!

MESSENGER

UNDER THE GREENWOOD TREE
WHO LOVES TO LIE WITH ME,
AND TURN HIS MERRY NOTE
UNTO THE SWEET BIRD'S THROAT.

COME HITHER, COME HITHER, COME HITHER:
HERE SHALL YOU SEE
NO ENEMY
BUT WINTER AND ROUGH WEATHER.

Somewhere during the song, Falstaff slips away, unseen to all. It is quiet and uneventful. He simply closes his eyes at some point, and sleeps, and is melted into air, into thin air.

HERE SHALL YOU SEE
NO ENEMY
BUT WINTER AND ROUGH WEATHER.

Othello checks on Falstaff. He goes to Mistress Quickly.

OTHELLO

He's gone, my lady.

QUICKLY

Say?

CLEOPATRA

Sir John, love. He's gone.

Pause.

QUICKLY

The breaking of so great a thing should have made a greater crack.

MESSENGER

(Beat. Then gently.) Shall I . . . let the Watchers, know, madam? They can . . . well . . .

QUICKLY

No, not yet, lad, not yet.

Pause.

CLEOPATRA

Would that the Author might write us out of this scene.

QUICKLY

He cannot write us out of it, 'twas he that wrote us into it; for we are the brief and abstract chronicles of the time -- and that we cannot alter. *(Beat.)* Sir John so often chid me, and bade me, 'With mirth and laughter let old wrinkles come.' Let us try to do so, and with grace.

(Beat.) We shall have a heavy miss of him, but come, good friends, for so you are; when time shall serve, there will be smiles again. *(To Messenger.)* I prithee, sing.

MESSENGER
SIGH NO MORE, DEAR ONES, SIGH NO MORE,
THE FATES ARE DECEIVERS EVER,
ONE FOOT IN SEA AND ONE ON SHORE,
TO ONE THING CONSTANT NEVER.

THEN SIGH NOT SO, BUT LET THEM GO,
AND BE YOU BLITHE AND BONNY,
CONVERTING ALL YOUR SOUNDS OF WOE
INTO HEY, NONNY NONNY.

SING NO MORE DITTIES, SING NO MORE
OF DUMPS SO DULL AND HEAVY.
THE FRAUD OF FATES WAS EVER SO,
SINCE SUMMER FIRST WAS LEAFY.

THEN SIGH NOT SO, BUT LET THEM GO
AND BE YOU BLITHE AND BONNY,
CONVERTING ALL YOUR SOUNDS OF WOE
INTO HEY, NONNY NONNY.
CONVERTING ALL YOUR SOUNDS OF WOE
INTO HEY, NONNY NONNY ...

End of Play

NOTES ON THE PLAY

The idea for this play came about in the very early days of the Covid pandemic. I had absolutely no desire to write about anything in those first few months. The world had turned topsy-turvy: the theater industry had shut down, we'd lost our jobs, our incomes, and a plague was overtaking our country. I was feeling lost and lazy and depressed, and also feeling guilty for feeling lost and lazy and depressed. I knew I should be writing, but I had no energy or inspiration to do so.

Then someone sent me a link to a magazine article. It was a story about how much writing Shakespeare had accomplished during the plague years of his time. His theaters had also been closed, but of course—Will being Will—he'd used the time to write *King Lear* and *Macbeth*, for god's sake.

Far from this article being inspiring—I'm embarrassed to say—it just pissed me off. I was dour and dark, and all I could think was, "Stop shaming me by telling me about all the great things a genius like Shakespeare accomplished during a 16th-century plague, okay?! Leave me alone. I'm not a genius, I'm depressed, and I'd like to stay that way, thank you very much. Our industry is gone, I'm unemployed for the foreseeable future, my friends are losing their apartments and struggling to buy groceries, cities are erupting in protests—why the hell would I write a play? Who would want to see a play that had anything to do with these times anyway?

"You know what I *should* write?!" I continued, still very pissy. "A story about a bunch of actors, like us, out of work, that's what I should write about. Or—no, *no*—wait, I've got it! Not *actors*, but a bunch of *characters* from plays that can't be acted any longer. Wait, even better, *Shakespearean* characters, like Falstaff and Mistress Quickly—yeah—and they're stuck in a bar somewhere—stuck in the goddamn Boar's Head Tavern—out of work, and struggling with the same issues we're all struggling with, and they're driving each other a little crazy because they've been cooped up together for so long, and—oh, just forget it! I'm not writing anything to make me feel more depressed than I am feeling right now. So, leave me alone. I'm going to have another cocktail far too early in the day than I should be having another cocktail."

I dismissed the idea and made myself a rye Manhattan.

The next morning, though . . . the idea was still there, lingering over in the corner . . .

Falstaff, sitting in a bar.
Alone.

And that was the beginning of the play. What would Falstaff do during the plague if he couldn't be with his companions? This man who embodied the Shakespearean adage, "With mirth and laughter let old wrinkles come!" This lover of good friends, good food and drink, and joy, and humor, and pranks? What would he do without Pistol and Poins to tease and carouse with? Without Bardolph, Nym and Pistol? What would happen if he wasn't able to cavort with Prince Hal and laugh out these difficult times together?

Hm . . . there could be something there.

Still, I wasn't completely convinced about the idea.

Then I remembered something I had read while working on *Dickens in America,* a one-man show I had written about Charles Dickens. It was a quote by his son, speaking about his father's writing habits:

And that was the real inspiration for me: I would write, in effect, *Shakespeare's Dream*. I would write a dream that Shakespeare was having during the plague, a dream in which his characters would dare to alter the great Author's text and "work out their histories in their way and not his."

This was the *improbable fiction* on which I'd hang the tale.

Crazy, I know. But there it is.

The lion's share of the dialogue in the play is made up of Shakespeare's own words. Culled and cannibalized from nearly all of his plays, I used many of them verbatim (in different contexts), but also adapted them, turned them on their heads, twisted them inside out, and reassigned them into the mouths of other characters from his plays. I also adapted language from archaic texts: 14th-century writings by Petrarch on the plague (which *literally* sounds like today's news); Samuel Pepys diaries (1665), Thomas Dekker's accounts of the plague (1603); and documents from the UK National Archives on the Great Plague, of which there are legions.

I started out to write a comedy. The first few drafts, therefore, did not dive very deeply into the darker happenings outside the world of The Boar's Head Tavern, into the reality of what was happening to London's population at that time: the struggles of the poor and under-represented; how those in power had abandoned the populace; how scores of the population ignored the curfews and laws against large gatherings, further exacerbating the spread of the disease (see Pepys diaries and UK National Archives on the Great Plague). How could I include social context like this in a comedy?

Many months later, however, when I began to work on subsequent drafts, our country had lost more than half a million people to the pandemic, many of whom might have been saved if we had had a semblance of humane or intelligent leadership. As Juliet says in the play: (adapted from a various 13th and 16th century texts concerning the plague in England and Sienna, Italy):

> "What a blemish on our fair nation;
> For it hath spotted our country with the stain
> Of cruelty and disregard; this,
> The subtle vapor of indifference,
> Kills more than the disease."

Life-altering events such as these literally change the words that come to mind while writing. The "little people," as R.L. Stevenson called them—or the muses, or the imagination—actually choose different nouns, different verbs; words that are more appropriate to the larger context of the life one is experiencing. The palette darkens, because the world has. Were I to ignore this, the play would be a lie. Yes, even within this funny, metaphysical, dream-like, *improbable* fiction . . . it would be a lie.

So I decided then that I would write a comedy, *mostly*. The final draft was, like all of us, greatly altered by the events of 2020-2021.

I tried to write a story that would be joyful and funny and loving and hurtful and maddening and heartbreaking and bewildering—as 2020 and beyond has been for so many of us—and I tried to write a story that, in the end, would be hopeful. For as Mistress Quickly reminds us in the play:

"When time shall serve, there will be smiles again."

THANKS

Thanks to American Players Theater for giving me the opportunity, and time, to workshop the play with a full cast and a director, early in 2020, and for eventually streaming it on PBS. Thanks also to APT for choosing the play to be the first production on their outdoor stage since the closing of the theaters in 2020.

Thanks to Brenda DeVita, Artistic Director of American Players Theater, and her artistic team, Jake Penner and Carey Cannon, for believing in the script and encouraging me to keep working on it.

Thanks to the wonderfully talented cast that premiered the play: Sarah Day, Brian Mani, Ronald Román-Meléndez, Chike Johnson, Tracy Arnold, and Melisa Pereyra. Each and every person in the room contributed greatly to the creation of this work, as did our stage manager, Evelyn Matten.

Many thanks to Tim Ocel, the director of the first production, who was on board with me from the first crazy idea, and through some very unpolished first drafts. His curiosity and theater artistry, and belief in the script, was a gift.

Heartfelt thanks to my friend and colleague, Gavin Lawrence, for daring me to write deeper, and for his trust in me that I could.

Thanks to my friend and artistic partner, Melisa Pereyra, who has challenged me to widen the lens through which I see the world and art ever since I first met her. Rigorous in the best of ways, I thank her for her artistry and her heart.

Many thanks to my wife, Brenda, who listened to me act out all the parts in our kitchen when I only had a few pages of a very rough script, and for telling me to keep writing; to Sara Young for her encouragement and generosity always—and her editing skills; to Todd Miller, Nancy Baenen, and James Bohnen for their encouragement and support in all my writing ventures; and a very special thanks to Arcadia Books.

ABOUT THE AUTHOR

James DeVita, a native of Long Island, NY, is an author, actor, and a theater director. He has worked as an actor in Japan, Germany, Australia, Ireland, and around the United States, and also worked as a fisherman on Long Island for five seasons.

Along with his novels, *A Winsome Murder, The Silenced, Blue,* and *Indifferent Red* (Fall 2021), Jim has also worked extensively as a playwright. His adult and produced plays for the stage include: *Christmas in Babylon, Learning to Stay, Gift of the Magi* (a musical adaptation); *In Acting Shakespeare; The Desert Queen* (the life of Gertrude Bell); *Dickens In America; Waiting for Vern,* and a new adaptation of *Cyrano de Bergerac.* His work for young audiences has been acknowledged with The Distinguished Play Award from The American Alliance of Theater and Education; The Intellectual Freedom Award by the Kentucky Council of Teachers of English/Language Arts; the Shubert Fendrich Memorial Playwriting Contest, and The American Alliance of Theater and Education honored his body of work with the Charlotte B. Chorpenning Award.

Jim is a recipient of the National Endowment for the Arts Literature Fellowship for Fiction, and a member of The Dramatists Guild and Actors Equity Association.

His education began as a first mate on the charter boat JIB VII out of Captree Boat Basin, NY, where he worked for five seasons. He then studied theater at Suffolk County Community College, Long Island, where he received an AS degree, and at the University of Wisconsin-Milwaukee, where he received a BFA. He also attended Madison Area Technical College where he was licensed as an Emergency Medical Technician. He lives in a small town in Wisconsin.